Parenting After Divorce For The Single Daddy

The Best Guide To Helping Single Dads Deal With Parenting Challenges After A Divorce

Nick Thomas

Copyright © 2015 Nick Thomas

All rights reserved

No part of this book may be reproduced in any form or by any electronic or mechanical means including information storage and retrieval systems, without permission in writing from the author. The only exception is by a reviewer, who may quote short excepts in a review.

Although the author and publisher have made every effort to ensure that the information in this book was correct at press time, the author and publisher do not assume and hereby disclaim any liability to any party for any loss, damage, or disruption caused by errors or omissions, whether such errors or omissions result from negligence, accident, or any other cause.

Visit my website at www.singledaddydating.com

ISBN-13: 978-1505359343

ISBN-10: 1505359341

JOIN OUR COMMUNITY!

Single Daddy Dating is a growing community of single fathers who look to help each other, not only with dating success but in all areas of their lives too. This includes parenting, career and finances advice.

Join us today and get '**10 Crucial Checklist To Dating Success For Single Fathers**' completely FREE!

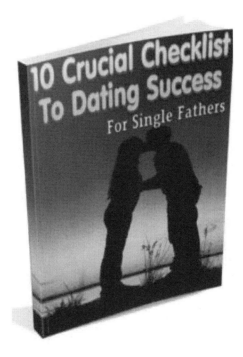

JOIN US AT
WWW.SINGLEDADDYDATING.COM/
NEWSLETTER/

NICK THOMAS   www.singledaddydating.com

CONTENTS

Chapter One: How Divorce Impacts Your Children And Dating Success.. 1

Chapter Two: Telling Your Child About The Divorce 26

Chapter Three: Common Mistakes Fathers Make When They Are Divorcing... 46

Chapter Four: Having A Parenting Plan....................... 66

Chapter Five: Why Family Meetings Matter................ 83

Chapter Six: Stop Blaming Your Ex-Wife 96

Chapter Seven: Seek Closure For The Sake Of The Child 110

Chapter Eight: Ex-Wife Getting Married 119

Chapter Nine: Introducing A New Partner To Your Child 129

Chapter Ten: Tough Conversations 138

Final Notes... 152

Chapter One: How Divorce Impacts Your Children And Dating Success

Divorce has become something very common in the past few years. Just a few decades ago, divorce was something which wasn't that common. Fast-forward now, everyone seems to know a divorced person.

The prevalence of divorce is so huge that many people are afraid to even get married in the first place. If you are someone who has been through a divorce, you know that a divorce impacts more than just the husband and wife.

From an estimation, it has been said that the divorce rate in the United States is 53%, United Kingdom 47%, Australia 43% and 36% in Japan. Every year, the divorce rate seem to be increasing. Even when the divorcees get a second or subsequent marriages, the chances of the next marriage being divorced would only increase.

We live in a time where the number of divorces continue to rise in most countries, and together with it, the cultural acceptance of it. Many adults and parents are completely unaware that there are many challenges when a divorce impact their children. Many books have been written and many studies done in the past few years regarding the huge impact that divorce has on children.

Regardless of what is said, it could be summarized that parents have a tremendous influence on the divorce both in the short and long term. In the United States alone, there are about 1.5 million children who will experience divorce every year.

As a parent, you wouldn't want to know that your actions are impacting your children negatively. However, the truth is it does. No parent who is going through a divorce wants the added anxiety and stress of knowing how they have negatively impact their children.

However, if you start to understand the potential negative impacts, the typical responses that the children would have and how to deal with it; you can help your children adjust to this huge change in their lives. As they learn to adapt to the situation, this ensures they wouldn't be completely affected by the divorce.

When going through a divorce, there is a tendency for many parents to completely focus on their own problems and start to blame their other spouse. They become self-absorbed with their problems, to a point where they fail to see what their children are going through. This only brings harm to the child.

When going through a divorce, co-operation between the two spouses is critical in ensuring that the child transitions well. Too many parents are so emotionally drained from the divorce and bring that emotional pain to their children too. When going through a divorce, it is common for the child to feel like he doesn't have enough time with his parents.

The most damaging aspect to the child is the lack of parental involvement by one or both of the parents with the children through the divorce.

When parents are not thinking about their own children's needs and emotional wellbeing, they run the risk of destroying the parent-child relationship. This increases the probability that the children will have future emotional and behavior problems. According to research, the following situations could impact the children:

- Children who have only one parent involved would have worse results compared to those children who have both parents. They also have higher graduation rates and less likely to drop out of school.

- Children who have constant and positive interactions with their parents have fewer health, emotional and other problems.

- Children living with a single parent would more likely live in poverty. This results in a higher possibility of being involved in gangs and criminal activities.

- Children that don't have a mother or father role model become more likely to engage in high-risk behaviour. This includes becoming sexually active earlier and causing teenage pregnancy.

From here, it should be clear that without dealing with the potential issues from a divorce, it causes tremendous problems for the child. These problems can be severe and becomes something that makes the relationship with your child hard to recover. Even if the parent realizes this in the future, it may be too late for them to do anything. The problem has already scarred the child to an extent where nothing can be done.

It isn't the divorce that causes stress in the child. Rather, the main cause for this is that their parents neglect them. They feel that the divorce has already broken up the family but now, they don't have anyone to depend on during this difficult period.

It is therefore important that both parents work together to ensure that there is a smooth transition in the divorce and for the years to come. This transition is important and should be done even before the divorce papers are signed.

How Children Respond To Divorce

Regardless of how old your children are, they will experience some effects from the divorce. Divorce is something that changes the dynamics of their life.

For the younger ones, they may not be able to express themselves verbally. However, you could still notice a change in behavior and other sort of tendencies as the child matures. For older children, they may tell you that they are alright with the divorce. However, they might feel torn and broken inside.

In general, children would go through a grief cycle when going through a divorce. Every child, depending on their personality, maturity and age; would respond differently. Their closeness to either parent would also impact their reaction towards the divorce.

Understanding their reactions towards the divorce is important if you want to help them. This chapter is about understanding the seven phases of how children respond to a divorce. As you understand these phases, you learn better what to expect in the future.

The following seven phases are what a child would normally experience during the divorce. These phases could possibly go on for about a year immediately after the divorce. All children express this differently, but the common reactions would include emotional and certain changes in behavior that could create tremendous problems for the parents.

Step 1: Denial

Denial is the first step. When your child is

aware that a divorce is pending, he might try to deny the fact. Those children who are in denial refuse to accept that their parents are getting a divorce. In this stage and throughout the divorce, the parents need to be as positive as possible about the other parent.

Make sure that you keep any explanations about the divorce and separation simple. Don't go into this process of trying to make yourself the victim. Don't go on blaming the other person or even yourself. Apologise to them, but don't dwell on self-pity. Focus instead on the basic things such as:-

- **Good and respectful comments about the other parent**. This is important because it shows that both you and your ex-wife are leaving on good terms. When you leave positive comments about your ex-wife, it shows that you still care for each other regardless of the divorce. This makes the child more comfortable with the situation.

- **Expression of love from the parent to the child**. This makes sure that the children feel secure despite the changes in their lives. This security is important because children often feel neglected during this difficult period.

- **The place where the child would live**. This should be discussed between you and your ex-wife before you even talk to your children about the divorce. This ensures that the child knows what to expect from the divorce.

- **A simple explanation about the divorce**. Keeping this simple ensures that your child wouldn't be confused about the reasons for the divorce. Always give them a reason so they won't overthink the situation.

The denial stage would be for different

lengths of time for different children. This depends on how mature the child is and how close they are to both parents. Understanding this stage is important so you don't react unnecessarily to any negative comments from them.

During this period, make sure that you spend as much time as possible with them to ensure they feel wanted. As much as they try to deny them, give them the time to accept the situation.

Step 2: Anger

After the denial, the next stage would be when the child feels angry about the divorce. This could be for a multitude of reasons. This anger may be directed at the parent for leaving home or for making a parent leave home. When this happens, you need to take time to explain to them with a simple explanation as like the first step.

From this explanation, it would allow him to quicker understand the situation. This makes him deal with his anger quicker. As you give him an explanation earlier in the divorce, it gives him the avenue for him to understand the situation.

During this stage, you can see many changes in him. He may look to express or suppress his anger in a multitude of ways. The anger that he has may also be due to other things such as:-

- Angry about the feelings of abandonment from their parents.

- Angry about the feelings of rejection from their parents.

- Angry at not having stability in his life. This commonly is because of the constant changes in his life.

Besides that, the child could also direct the anger to himself. He may feel that he was the one who caused the divorce. This sort of anger is known as 'guilt' – which is feeling anger towards oneself.

Such guilt need to be treated by telling him it is not his fault. Should you fail to do that, it would end up in him being immobilized in the future. He may feel unworthy and constantly afraid to try anything in the future for fear of messing up.

During this stage, you also need to allow him to feel his anger. Don't try to fight that anger. Rather, you should embrace it. He may do some terrible things such as using violence in school but you need to be calm.

Just remind yourself that he is going through a difficult period as well. He may be angry because of the divorce. Look to channel his anger towards something else like sports. Involve him in other activities so he can forget about things. Sports is great because he is able to tire himself and become healthier as well.

Step 3: Anxiety

Anxiety is a very common effect in a divorce. The child wouldn't be able to express it in words, but you could see a big change in his behavior. You could find him having emotional outbursts at members of the family or towards other children at school.

This stage can be for a longer period than the first two stages. The child may feel afraid and insecure about the situation all the time. They feel anxious because they don't have emotional safety that a child needs. Besides that, this anxiety could also result in other health issues. They would find it hard to eat or sleep regularly and constantly complain of headaches and fatigue. Generally, the fatigue comes about because they are constantly thinking all the time. Their thoughts create emotional tension, thus the anxiety.

During this period, it is important that you spend time making the child feel comfortable. Generally, it is hard to avoid dealing with this step when he is anxious. In fact, this depends a lot on your relationship with your children before the divorce in the first place. If you are someone who always ensures that your child is safe, this stage may pass by quickly. This may include talking to him or giving him attention. However, if your child doesn't feel safe in the first place, this stage may take longer.

This is a reason why you should talk things through with your wife before you even tell your children about the divorce. This helps reduce the potential anxiety. You would learn more about this in the next chapter.

Step 4: Confusion

Children would tend to get very confused about what is happening during the divorce. This is another result of the insecurity of the divorce and its subsequent changes.

If possible, try to keep the common routines and predictability between being in your house and your ex-wife's house. Try to give them some structure. A good way to do this is to use text messages and email reminders to keep your children informed of what they need to know regarding their time with their mother and you. Also be clear about who would pick them up and where they would go after school or during the weekends.

You would also need to answer many of their questions from time to time. They would be filled by questions about what has happened. Although it can be very frustrating for you to answer them, you need to try your best to answer all their questions. Even if you don't have good answers to their questions, make sure that you are there to listen to them all the time.

Dealing with the child's confusion is difficult for you, because you may be confused about the situation as well. You feel that the divorce has caused some emotional turbulence. As such, it is sometimes recommended that you allow your child to speak to some third party about it. It may be a school counsellor or a therapist. They may be able to make your child more comfortable with the situation.

Step 5: Bargaining

During this phase, the children would go through a phase where they try to bargain with their parents. They want to try to make sure that the divorce doesn't happen. This stage is different for different children. Some children may not go through this stage while some would be very stubborn. They would try to make sure that they do their best to ensure that divorce doesn't happen.

This is when they are still in strong denial about the situation. They may try to ensure all the siblings put in effort to reunite the family. This child would pull together other siblings to make you guilty or spark back the connection that you have with your ex-wife.

During this situation, you may feel touched because he/she would put in so much effort to ensure that the marriage continues. However, you need to make it clear to your children that they didn't cause the divorce and as such, they can't 'fix' it. It may be very disheartening to have to tell them that though.

They may even bargain with a higher power like God, to bring their family together. During my meeting with single fathers, one of them mentioned that his daughter prayed every day to try reunite the family. It didn't happen but he felt so guilty throughout the period. This is a reaction that you need to deal with though. Different children react to different stages in their own ways.

Step 6: Depression

When going through a divorce, it is natural that a child feels they lack a certain joy. They find it difficult to find the positive in things. You may find them not wanting to do their normal day-to-day activities such as their hobbies or even their daily homework. As such, their results in school suffer.

Even though this is the toughest stage to go through, you need to encourage your child to stay involved and active. At all times, encourage him or her to do more activities. These activities may be more than just sports. It can also involve some club activities or meeting up with friends more often.

However, you should ensure that they are with positive friends that set a good role model. As much as you shouldn't invade their privacy, you must take time to know who they hang out with. Very often, children hang out with other bad influences during this difficult period.

Be positive and stay focused on the future. Paint a wonderful future for them. Both you and your wife need to let the children know that although things would be different, they would still be loved and cared for. If the depression becomes worse, you need to talk to a physician. Very often, speaking to a third party can make all the difference.

The third party can be a close family member or a professional therapist. In many situations, talking to a third party is more comfortable for your child than talking to you. He may feel more comfortable opening up about the situation and this allows him to get to the next step much faster.

Step 7: Acceptance

As time passes, your child would slowly learn to accept the situation. Like said, this depends a lot on the child's maturity and how much effort you put in. He would accept that the divorce is going to happen or has happened. He would still see your wife as his mother and you as his father. Given time, you need to believe that your children would adjust to the divorce.

For most children, this would take about a year to reach full acceptance of the situation. This includes understanding how to communicate with both parents and the co-parenting plan, which you would learn about in future chapters. However, you need to make sure that there is as little conflict and negativity as possible. The less of such situations that the children experience, the faster it would take them to accept the divorce.

Acceptance is the main target that you as a parent should aim for. You are looking for them to accept the divorce as a part of their life. This is your main aim as a divorced parent. The divorce would change things, but you would look to make his life as normal as possible and that you still love him.

***

Understanding these seven steps is important to ensure that you understand better how children would react. These steps are mere generalization of what children would normally go through.

The time taken for each child in different stages would be different. Some children spend longer or shorter time in some stages.

As you understand these steps, you are in a better position to deal with your children during the divorce.

Deal With The Divorce Before You Date

When speaking to many single fathers, I am surprised by how many actually don't have their affairs in order. Many of them want to date other women, but they still have plenty of other things on their mind. This ranges from their emotionally troubled children, bothersome ex-wife or unsettled careers.

It would be difficult for me to say that you can completely get your affairs in order. Things are never stable. However, you should ensure that the main areas in your life are as stable as possible. This includes your parenting, dealing with the divorce proceedings and having a stable career. This ensures that you have peace of mind when you start dating again. Dating is something that could take away a lot from yourself. If you don't have the confidence in yourself yet, you may find that dating can drag you emotionally.

Never underestimate how having some stability in life would help your dating success. When a single father meet other women, he want to be able to give her time and attention. It is hard for you to do so if you are bothered by petty things all the time. Before you date, you should look to plan your affairs well.

From experience, single women want a stable man and not someone who is full of emotional baggage. They don't want someone who is constantly worried when they go out on a date. As such, it is my general recommendation to keep your affairs in order first.

Perhaps the biggest impact towards your dating success is having your children being alright about it. If your children are alright with you dating, you are able to have some peace of mind. They know that it is your own life and you have the right to do what you want.

That is why you need to give them some stability in their lives after the divorce. Ensure that there are some routine in their daily affairs and that everything is taken care of. This is what this book is all about – to ensure that you have everything taken care before you start dating, and this starts from making sure that you have your children in order.

From this future chapters, you would learn about how to help your children deal with the divorce and parenting them in the future. In the next chapter, you learn a big aspect about ensuring that you parent your children well after the divorce. This is regarding how to tell them about the divorce.

Chapter Two: Telling Your Child About The Divorce

Perhaps the toughest thing that I have done in life is to talk to my children about the divorce. I can never forget the nervousness and anxiety I had to face. I imagined my daughters crying and being angry at me. It played on my mind endlessly before I started to tell them about it.

Needless to say, it will probably be tough on you too. You would be worried about how your child would react. Would they be angry?

Would they feel sad? Your mind is filled with a million possibilities on how they would possibly react.

When I was about to tell my daughter about the impending divorce with my wife, I felt a shudder at the thought of it. I didn't know how she would react. In fact, I remember feeling that I didn't want to continue with the divorce because I didn't want to tell my children about it. That was the amount of fear that I have.

I managed to pull through. I managed to sit them down and talk to them about it. Trust me, it was tough. I have never felt so ashamed about myself in my life. I felt that I have let my children down tremendously. However, it had to be done. In retrospect, telling them is probably the best thing that I have done. I managed to be completely vulnerable in front of them. I showed them that I have flaws too. My second daughter was angry with me initially, but she managed to accept it as time passes.

In fact, when going through a divorce, you may be surprised that most children would already have some knowledge about it. This is especially for the older children. They may have already been expecting a divorce and may be less surprised or angry than you would have expected. In fact, they would come up with several questions for you. This include:-

- How it would change his life?
- Do you still love her (your ex-wife)?
- Where will the child live?
- Do you hate each other?
- Do you still love me?
- When will I spend time with the other parent

And many more…

If you look into the nature of these questions, you can sense that the child is seeking for some security. They want a certain sense of security in their life, before the divorce happens. They want a feeling of love, reassurance and support. From these conversations with your child, you would likely be able to give it to them. You want to reassure them that they are still loved and they have all the support they need.

Ideally, you should look to talk to your wife about the divorce first. Make sure you have discussed everything and considered every possibility. This is important to ensure that you know how to answer your child in the best possible manner. You should also discuss what information both of you wish to share with regards to the divorce. When dealing with a divorce, the children wants to know about two main things:-

- Why the divorce has happened?

- Anything relating to their life in the future. How it changes their lives?

However, you need to be ensure that you don't tell them too much. Your children shouldn't be told about these following issues:-

- Any negativity concerning your wife
- Any negative feelings you have about the other parent
- What caused the divorce
- Any betrayal in the marriage

This depends a lot on the age of the child. Older children tend to ask more mature questions. However, you shouldn't get involved in any negativity or bash the other parent.

That is why you should discuss with your wife first to ensure consistency in the answers.

Should the both of you be consistent with your answers, the children understands that both of you aren't going to talk about the negative aspects of the divorce. As such, the child wouldn't feel conflicted or angry with the other parent.

The tendency many parents have is to ignore the divorce talk as it can prove to be uncomfortable for them. However, this is an important part of divorce. If at all possible, try to talk to your children about the divorce together with both you and your wife. This ensures that the children and parents hear the similar information. Having mixed information would increases the anxiety and confusion throughout the process of divorce.

You can also get a mediator or advisor to help this process. At times, a family therapist, counsellor or other members of the family could be the 'middle person' in the discussion. This person would be emotionally calm and able to stabilise the emotions. The children would thus be more comfortable with the situation.

Accept Their Feelings

During the discussion, it should be expected that there would be some negative reaction from your children. It is important that you accept them as it comes about. If they are angry, allow them to be angry. If they are disappointed, allow them some space to feel sad. For children to go through such a situation can be difficult. You need to allow them to express themselves in their own ways.

Let them be open towards you. Should they ask you anything, don't push it aside. Accept it and look to find a way to reassure them about the situation. The most important thing now is to care about not only the facts but rather their feelings as well. Find for ways to reassure them.

They won't be able to accept the situation immediately when they tell you. In fact, if it seems that they can accept the situation immediately, it can be an indication of something bad. It may be an indication that they are suppressing their emotions. This isn't a good thing at all as you want them to be able to open up their feelings.

You need to give them some time to get used to the situation. Give them some space until they are ready to accept the situation. In communication, one of the most critical skills is to listen actively to the other person. This is the process of using the powers of observation and attentive listening to understand what the other person is saying and meaning. This is especially important for children who have trouble expressing themselves with words.

You should be aware of the possible signs of stress, anxiety and distraction when talking about the divorce. This may indicate that the child isn't ready to openly talk about it yet. Active listening helps tremendously during this situation. During this process of active listening, you should look to:-

- Turn off every electronic device such as the television, handphone, and computer. Everything distracting should be avoided.

- Talk to the child in a comfortable environment.

- Never criticise the child or make him feel uncomfortable about the situation.

- Encourage him to communicate and express himself openly. Look to validate their emotions whether it is negative or positive.

- Ask non-judgmental questions to ensure that the child is clearer about the situation.

When dealing with this situation, the child would feel uncertain about his future. He isn't sure what would happen to his daily affairs. From the divorce, there is a possibility that he would have to move to another state and lose his friends. Many things changes and he isn't ready for it. As such, he may be acting up and make things difficult for you.

It is therefore crucial to stay focused on the future. Look to end the conversations about how the future would be. This is important because it gives the child a vision about how the future would be.

It would take some time for you to talk to your child about the past and the present. Look to talk openly about both you and your wife's relationship with the children. Make sure that it continues to improve and that you stay positive in the future.

Children are really perceptive and they would take cue from how the parents talk to each other. As such, always set a positive example for your children.

You should definitely allow your child to have a say about the future that they want to have. Let them have some input. Children love it when they know that their opinions are being heard by adults. Make sure that you ask them about the activities that they want to do. Instead of focusing on the past, focus on the future and create activities that you could enjoy with your children.

Different Age Children React Differently

Children of different ages may be more mature or immature than others in their age group. However, it could be said that there is a general consensus on how children normally react at different ages. In this part, you would learn how children of different ages would react.

Knowing how different children react to a divorce is important. You get to understand what to look out for before you tell them about it. Remember that this is just an assumption of the situation. This doesn't mean that all children act in the same way. This is a simple stereotyping of how children of different ages react.

Infant To Five Years Old

Children of this age might not able to realise any changes and as such, they would be able to go through the divorce very easily. They can easily accept the changes. In fact, they might not even be aware about the changes from the divorce.

However, for some sensitive children, they might display some grief as they get older. Even if the divorce has passed years later, they may experience the after-effects only later. There are certain children who are more sensitive who can sense the changes. At about the age of two years old, children would start to develop a sense of trust and an understanding of the world and their environment. When such changes happen, they feel like they don't have certainty. This would lead to tantrums and other emotional frustrations.

Parents of that age need to constantly have a steady routine between your house and your wife's house. Ideally, the child should be able to communicate with both parents each day. This could be done over a webcam on the internet. The more they realise that they have a mother and father, they would feel more secure and loved. This is an important stage in a baby's development.

Another great way is to ensure that there are photographs of the entire family in the house. Make sure that you have such photographs that shows you and your wife, together with other siblings. It is important that the parent who have the most parenting time (normally the mother) talk about the other parent frequently to the child. This makes sure that the child feels certain about the future because he has both parents. You make sure that the child has memories of the other parent if you get more parenting time.

Six To Nine Years Old

During this age, children are known as "parent pleasers". They want to know that their parents feel good about them. They want their parents to be happy and proud of them. During this time, the child tend to talk with one parent more than the other. As such, it is normal that the child would be closer to another parent.

It is important that you allow the child to talk about the various positive aspects about your ex-wife. You should try to make them feel good about the other parent. Avoid any sarcasm and unnecessary questioning as it causes the child to feel uncomfortable. Many man who have yet to get through their divorce ask their children incessantly about their ex-wives. This isn't something that is healthy for the child as it makes him uncomfortable.

By being there to be positive about their mothers, their feelings would be validated. It is very likely when going through a divorce that children this age would feel sad. They feel lonely and helpless.

Take time to listen to them without any judgment. This is important as it makes them feel validated. If it is tough, find a counsellor who works specifically with children. Being able to talk to a stranger about their emotions would greatly enhance their well-being.

Ten To Twelve Years Old

Children in this age range tend to be the group that are most affected from the divorce. This is for multiple reasons. However, the main issue is that they are struggling with their own identity. They have yet to be teenagers and such, they have to deal with tremendous emotional changes. A divorce can result in them feeling rejected or betrayed.

When children this age hear of any problems in the family, they tend to be more sensitive than other age group. They have known enough to understand certain situations, but they don't have the emotional maturity to handle the emotions that arise.

When you are arguing with your wife and the atmosphere becomes hostile, they can pick up on the negativity and may feel terrible about it. From this, the child could react in many ways. This impacts his school life tremendously. During this period, he/she might decide who the 'bad one' in the divorce is. This lack of emotional maturity means that he would try to find for the bad one in the marriage. He may point the finger at the bad one – either you or your ex-wife.

This results in the child trying to 'move away' from the parent that he feels is the bad one. He would see you or your wife as at fault for the divorce. This isn't healthy because the child may feel a deep sense of resentment towards that parent. Ultimately, this only hurts the child because children need to have both parents to be able to grow successfully as a person.

Even if the child thinks that your ex-wife is at fault, you should look to full encourage a positive relationship between the child and your wife. If you encourage such communication, the child would feel that he is cared for. This helps his development in the future. He would be more willing to engage with your wife and this helps maintain a loving relationship.

If he blames you though, you need to talk to your ex-wife on how to deal with the situation. You are not doing it to feel better about yourself, but rather to make sure that your child can grow up in a better environment.

Thirteen To Nineteen Years Old

Older children tend to respond to divorce in a more mature way. There are typically two sort of responses:-

- See the divorce between the parents, but continue to have a good relationship with both of them.

- Blame one parent and refuse to interact with that parent.

Similarly, it is crucial that you encourage and facilitate the child's interaction between you and your ex-wife. It doesn't matter if it is just a brief interaction. This simple interaction can mean a lot to your child.

Very often, the older child may try to help out with the situation. It is important that the child don't see themselves as being responsible for the divorce. You must also ensure that they don't feel responsible for the well-being of their other siblings.

During this period, they may try to volunteer around the family more, but they shouldn't be obligated to help out. You need to remember that your child is still a child. You can't force him/her to grow up. They still need time for themselves. They still have friends and other activities in their life.

You need to be there for children of this age. Make sure that they have the freedom to talk to each parent. Make time to spend with each child every day, talking about what is happening in their life. Ask them about any potential issues in their lives. During this age, many children tend to keep things to themselves. Therefore, don't force them to speak up to you if they don't want to.

It is common for the child to be closer to one parent. If the child is closer to you, make it a point to talk positive things about your wife. You should also encourage communication and for your child to meet up with their mother all the time.

If the child is closer to your wife, you need to talk to your wife and try to encourage more positivity in the conversation. Tell her that you need to spend some time with your child too. Ensure that you are able to spend some quality time so that the child would be able to know you too.

Chapter Three: Common Mistakes Fathers Make When They Are Divorcing

Post-divorce parenting is filled with many considerations due to it being a highly emotionally-tensed period. During post-divorce parenting, many parents don't realize how it could impact the long term standing in the parenting relationship. If not done right, it can change the entire course of your parenting. Failing to do it right will cause them to be distant themselves from you.

Louis from Manhattan mentioned the same thing. After his divorce, he end up spending a lot of time on work. He needed to drown himself at work because he needed a way to forget about the divorce. During this period, he wasn't there for his two children. His children were in their teenage years and he allowed his ex-wife to decide on everything that has to do with parenting.

He regretted this decision as he got older. As the years passed by, his children didn't want to be around him. He struggled to have any meaningful conversation whatsoever with his children. He may have a successful career now, but he regrets that he can't have a fulfilling relationship with them. He notes that post-divorce is a situation that can be very vulnerable for the children. If you don't do it right, you may regret it forever.

The divorce has already impacted your children. If you don't do the right thing to fix the parent-child relationship, it brings about extra damage on top of the pain from the divorce. Without realizing it, some parents become too self-absorb that they neglect their children. Having said that, if you take time to understand the common mistakes that are made, you can avoid them.

Biggest Mistakes In Post-Divorce Parenting

From experience, these are the common mistakes that are being made by single fathers. These mistakes help prevent newly-divorced man from making the mistakes that may haunt them for the rest of their lives. Among the mistakes are:-

- **Forcing Your Child To Choose A Side.** Whenever there is a conflict in anything, you may try to make the child choose sides. This may be a simple thing such as scheduling or some other complicated matter such as allowing your child to date. For example, your ex-wife may not allow your son to date and you take the opportunity of it. You tell him that it is alright to date, just to make your wife the 'bad parent'.

- **Sabotaging Your Child's Relationship With Your Wife**. This is common because you want to make your wife the cause of the divorce. You have yet to get over her and the easy thing to do is to blame her for everything that has happened. You say bad things about what she has done during the divorce. This makes your child hate your ex-wife.

- **Get Information About Your Wife From Your Children**. This is common because you want to know how your wife is doing. However, placing your child in the middle of the both of you only makes him confused about the situation. There are men who want to behave like they are over their spouse but try to gain some information about their wives from the children. This makes the child feel uncomfortable because they don't like spreading gossip.

- **Using Your Child As A Pawn**. Many people try to get back at their ex-wife by using their children. They try to make their ex-wives guilty by their children's actions. This may be prompting their child to ask the ex-wife about certain things. The man knows that the ex-wife is sensitive about some things are would prompt the child to question the ex-wife. This makes her uncomfortable.

- **Transferring Frustrations**. There are times where men get frustrated with their children because their children resembles their ex-wife. It could be a daughter that looks similar to the ex-wife. He would scold her and look for mistakes all the time.

- **Companion And Support**. There are some fathers who depend on their children for companion and support due to their loneliness. This is dangerous for the child because you could become overly dependent on the child. You would want to be with them all the time, while invading their privacy. Over a period of time, they are afraid to mix around with you because you are so attached to them.

- **Treating Your Child As An Adult**. Because you aren't readily available to do many things, you treat your child like an adult so that he could support you. This is mainly because you are emotionally vulnerable. This is dangerous if your child is still young. You may end up putting too much pressure on him to be someone he is not. Over time, the child would be afraid of being with you.

- **Family Events**. Some men try to make family events into pressure cookers when their ex-spouse are around. They make it as uncomfortable as possible for their ex, not realising that it would also make it difficult for their children and other people. Such events might include birthdays, school programs and holidays.

- **Becoming Emotionally Needy**. When the child wants to spend time with the ex-wife or other members of the family, the father may try to make the child feel guilty about it. This is because he is dependent on the child to feel good. This makes the child uncomfortable and guilty should he spend time with other people. He would be thinking about you and try to relieve you of your neediness.

- **Satisfying Every Material Desires.** During this period, you may feel guilty about the divorce. To get over this feeling, you try to buy your child every material indulgence you could. This becomes an extremely bad thing as your child could end up being a spoilt brat. He may also use the divorce as a way of getting things from you in the future.

These mistakes are common and you should look to avoid it. However, it is easier said than done when you are emotionally vulnerable. To do so, you need to discuss with your wife about a parenting plan. This is covered in the next chapter.

The importance of this stage cannot be understated. You need to know that regardless of how difficult people work to be co-parents, there would be certain traps and communication issues between you and your ex-wife. As you understand the possible problems and traps that arise from co-parenting, you could bring it up during the discussion with your ex-wife. This avoids having your children getting involved in misunderstandings, conflict and negativity from the divorce.

Even if you are a great communicator with other people, there are times during the discussion where you become negative about the situation. The moment you become defensive, you stop listening to the other person and become focused on defending yourself. You try to defend yourself with a remark from what you have heard from your ex-wife.

If you find yourself being defensive because of what she has said, try to understand your own reactions. You should take time to calm yourself and get back on track. You can tell her that you need some time to consider her comments. Just tell her that you need a short break.

During this break, take a few deep breaths to calm down. Think deeply about what the other person has said and try to understand why you are in a defensive mode. Address it honestly so that you can put it behind you and listen when the conversation restarts. You need to understand that being defensive is a natural emotional method of protecting ourselves from things that we don't want to hear. There are certain times where this is valid but for certain situations, it may not be true at all.

Simply arguing with your ex-wife won't solve anything. Besides, it would only be counterproductive in creating a collaborative atmosphere for effective parenting. The key thing to focus isn't on who is right but rather to keep your child out of any conflict. You need to keep it clear with your ex-wife that the focus is to make your child's life better, not on arguing over who is right.

Children Being Adults

There would be a time where your children would try to act as adults during the communication with the parents. This is common because the child would feel that he/she needs to "step up" to try to improve the situation.

The child would try to become a mediator between the parents. He would try to help calm the situation or may even try to get the both of you to make amends with each other. Besides that, he could also act as a caregiver or supporter for either parents.

During this period, it is important to prevent children from playing these roles as it could lead to anxiety and stress. This makes it difficult for the relationship with your child over a period of time.

The thing about divorce is that most of the parenting issues doesn't revolve around the children. In fact, most of them are issues that are not open to debate or approval of the children. If parents allow children to make a decision or mediate parent conflicts, it creates a very damaging aspect on the divorce.

Parents should look to make important life decisions together. You don't need the make those decisions with the approval of your children. However, you should look to take into consideration their opinions about the matter. The following questions are what you should not ask your children about:-

- Where they want to live – with which parent?

- When they would want to meet up with the other parent?

- How much time they would like to spend with each parent?

- Would they want their siblings to go with them to meet the other parent?

- What they dislike about the other parent or her new partner?

- Who they would like to live with?

Asking them these questions may set them up for unhappiness. When you give them a choice in such situations, it may seem like you are being a 'democratic' parent. However, this isn't wise. You wouldn't want your child to have a say in everything because this makes them unhappy if you have asked them for their opinions but they didn't get it their way. Instead, both you and your ex-wife should discuss this together, leaving out your children.

At times, children would try to avoid such questions because they know it could trigger an angry response from the parent. They may simply tell you something just to please you. However, even if they tell you something that disappoints you, you have to be able to control your emotions.

Children would also ask you certain questions. You need to take note on the issues that your children bring up with you. You need to observe what topics that aren't being readily discussed and see how you can bring it up with them.

Don't ask them about why they bring certain questions up. Even if it is uncomfortable, you should look to always answer their questions. Talk to them and assure them that you would think of a way of dealing with the situation. If you can't find a solution straight away, tell them that you need some time. Remember to go back to them and answer their questions. Don't forget it and treat it like it never happen. The child might remember this and not open up to you in the future.

When dealing with the issue, work with the other parent. This ensures that both of you have a complete picture about the entire situation. You can get her opinion to see what happens in the future. It is also important to maintain congruency. This ensures that both parents come out with a similar answer when they are asked about something. You wouldn't want your ex-wife to answer something differently from you. This only creates confusion for the child.

Children Being Spies

In many cases, you may not want to deal directly with your ex-wife because you are afraid of unsettling her. As such, you ask your child to send the message for you. This isn't wise as it has a potential to create conflict. It creates a situation where the message wouldn't be relayed correctly or completely. This only leads to increased tension between you and your ex-wife.

Regardless of how difficult it is to talk directly to your ex-wife, you should never use your children to send messages to her. When you place such a responsibility on your child, the ex-wife may end up being angry with them. Perhaps you have send a message that makes your ex-wife unhappy. The child would then perceive that it is him that has causes your ex-wife to be unhappy.

You can consider using email or probably a text message to communicate possible issues with your ex-wife. This is especially for issues that she might get angry with.

This allows them to think about what you have to say and also has time to think about how they want to respond. This ensures that the child is out of the situation.

Many fathers also try to use their children as spies. They want to know how their ex-wife is doing. They want to find out if she is dating another person, how she is holding up or whether she is looking for a job. When you put your child responsible to find out such answers, you make them feel tensed when they are with you. Such a situation presents a real moral dilemma for them.

Part of them feel that they aren't supposed to tell the other parent. However, another part of them feel that they should be open with their parents. When this situation happens, they could end up being closed up to you. They would try avoid talking to ensure that this dilemma doesn't happen.

Should you have any personal questions, you need to ask your ex-wife directly. Make sure that your child isn't present. If your ex-wife isn't comfortable sharing those information with you, then move on. If she shares those information with you, accept them and move on.

Either way, you should try to exclude your children from any communication between you and your ex-wife. You can talk to your children to get their opinions about certain issues, but you should never give them the power to make decisions directly.

Financial Issues

Perhaps the most difficult part of going through a divorce is that there would be a decrease in disposable income. You may need to pay child support or alimony payments. This would not only be in the immediate effect but also be the same for the next few years from then.

When dealing with the issue of money, you must make sure that you don't bring your children into it. Try to keep it as far away as possible. Despite the possible tensions of money with your ex-wife, you need to stay calm. Make sure that you have discussed the issue of money with her to ensure that it doesn't spill over to parenting your children. Among the issues that would possibly affect the children include:-

- Child support payments

- Funds for the basic needs of the child. This may be a situation where there is a lack of funds.

- Financial stress and concerns that you have as a parent. This includes mortgage and car loan payments.

These are the few things you must discuss with your child. This includes the fact that you have to save on certain things. This may include not being able to eat out or not ordering food. Tell your child that you need to save on many things. Mature children might be able to understand and help you save.

You can also discuss about the allowance you pay your child. You would need to discuss with your ex-wife about it. Make sure it is clear on who would pay him as well as the amount of allowances. Many times when a parent try to buy the child's heart, he/she may look to give them more money. Make sure both of you don't overpay the allowance as this makes your child spend on unnecessary things. That being said, don't underpay your child as he might hold a grudge towards either of you.

Try to reassure the child that you have things under control when it comes to your finances. Even if things are difficult, make sure they feel secure about the situation. Work harder if you have to, but try to make them feel safe. This allows them to focus better on their studies, making friends and enjoying their younger years.

Chapter Four: Having A Parenting Plan

When going through a divorce, people don't make the best decisions and tend to act impulsively. You feel hurt and betrayed. You feel that the future look gloomy. As this time can be difficult for parents, sitting down and taking the time to talk things with your ex-wife would help things tremendously.

Writing a plan for raising the child that both parents could follow assist both you and your wife start the co-parenting process and respect each other's role in the well-being of the child.

However, you should first understand the different parenting models that have been researched on. Since divorce is something that is so common these days, researchers have conducted evaluations to determine the different parenting styles and how they impact the children.

These different styles allow you to understand why having a parenting plan can be so important. Make sure that you understand the pros and cons of each parenting approach before you start off with creating your parenting plan. Ideally, be clear to your ex-wife about how you plan to approach parenting the child or children.

Models Of Parenting

From the research which is being done, there

are generally three types of parenting models. These would be discussed and explained in a manner to ensure that you understand how these models impacts your children. Generally, the three common models are:-

(1) Co-Parenting Model

(2) Parallel Parenting Model

(3) Independent Parenting Model

Co-Parenting Model

This model is the best because it is the most child-friendly. This is known as 'co-parenting' because it means that both parties play an important role in parenting the child.

In this model, you and your ex-wife would actively discuss any potential issues related to your child or children. Both of you would routinely talk to each other about the child.

This means that you take the time to talk either face-to-face or on the phone. There are a set of concerns about the child that both of you actively seek to share opinions and discuss about things.

While you and your ex-wife might not specifically spend time with your child together, you can make it a priority to be there together for important functions. Such functions might include birthday parties, school events or any other important activities. The main thing is to make the child feel supported and loved in whatever activities they do. The child would feel that both his parents place him as a very important part in their lives.

For many divorced parents, co-parenting might sound too difficult. They might feel that the tensions between both of them are too much for them to handle because they find it hard to talk to each other. This is especially when one parent had been betrayed in the marriage. However, many professionals are of the opinion that this model is the best model for parenting your child.

This is why the interaction between you and your ex-wife is important. Make it clear that you are not doing it for each other but rather for the child. Both parents should remain respectful and child-centred during such interactions.

Co-parenting doesn't mean that you have to be all-happy with your ex-wife. It simply means that you focus on the child's happiness, health, development and well-being and forget about the past.

For this model to work, both parents have to play an important role. Whatever that has happened in the past has to be put aside. Communication between the two parents should be solely on bringing up the child. There might be certain frustrations, but effective parenting with this model brings up the best situation for your child to be in. Look to eliminate any anger that you have towards each other in the presence of the child.

Parallel Parenting Model

In this model, you would find that there are limited interaction between the two parents. This is a model that is often use directly after the divorce has happened. This means that both parents are focused on achieving the same goals for their children.

To put this clearly, both the parents are heading towards the same direction. Parallel parenting requires that the parents have a common understanding as to what the other is doing with regards to the children. They simply ensure that they are doing the same things.

However, there is limited communication

between the two parents. The child will still have certain routine and predictability in their day-to-day life.

When using such a model, it is common for parents to have a written parenting plan. This helps to outline the various aspects of raising the child.

This includes a detail scheduling of the parenting time, routines, medical issues, discipline and extra financial aspects which affects the child.

Using this model, the parents communicate through an attorney or therapists. This ensures that everything remain civil.

In a way, parallel parenting helps to ensure that the child gets a sense of certainty. Although the relationship between you and your ex-wife isn't completely healed, there is still a sense of shared goals.

Independent Parenting

In such an arrangement, each parent would have their own way of doing things. They each have their own rules, expectations and daily routines when it comes to the children. When their children go to visit either of them, the children would need to adapt to the different parent. In such a setup, both parents don't consult each other to create a set way of dealing with things.

Parents who are observant would be able to see the problems with this parenting model. Among the problems of such a parenting model includes:-

- **They become bad communicators**. In such a model, the children don't have the chance to see their parents working together. They can see that their parents are in conflict and not interacting well. This teach them the wrong communication skills.

- **They may try to take advantage of the situation.** When the child see such a situation, they may try to take advantage of the situation. They may see that their parents are not talking. The child may be living two different lives and don't have the ability to talk about what is happening in the other home.

- **Lack of predictability.** When growing up, all children need a certain predictability and structure. Such a parenting model may not help with this, especially if you and your ex-wife have different methods of parenting. The child would be confused if the rules and expectations are extremely different between you and your ex-wife's home.

- **They become 'actors'.** Due to the fact that the children need to adapt to different parents, they may try to be someone else to please each parent. While a parent might disallow something, the other parent might allow it. This means that a sense of right and wrong isn't instilled. Rather, the focus is on pleasing their parents.

This parenting model may exist in certain divorces that are tensed where both parents find it hard to talk at all. However, this isn't a good model for a child's development. You would need to work with a family therapist or parenting coordinator to get the communication on track.

Which Parenting Model?

The parenting model that is suitable for you and your ex-wife depends a lot on how well you get along with her. In bringing up emotionally health children, you need to bring them up to the **Co-Parenting Model**. This is the best. However, it could be difficult sometimes. Some divorce end up messy that it solely becomes a Parallel or Independent Model.

During the various stages of your divorce, a different model might also apply. However, you need to try to focus on making it into a Co-Parenting Model. This takes great communication skills and you would need to deal with your emotions beforehand. As such, a great thing to accommodate this is to have a parenting plan.

What Is A Parenting Plan

In most divorce, it is always recommended to have a parenting plan. A parenting plan is an actual component of a divorce mediation strategy and is filed with the court to show the methods where the parents have agreed to go about with parenting the child or children.

Even if there are certain states where a

parenting plan isn't required by law, it is still a helpful way to ensure there are certain consistency, stability and routine in bringing up a child. From the previous chapters, it should be clear why this is important. This is not only for the immediate time period after the divorce, but for the years to come as well.

In creating the parenting plan, it is best for you to work with the ex-wife one-on-one. However, this might be difficult in certain situations. As such, it is better if you have parenting co-ordinators, lawyers or mediators to help both of you come out with a plan.

A parenting plan could include a handwritten document or a template-type document that you could get from the internet. Ideally, it should be as detailed as possible. This ensures that there wouldn't be any misunderstanding and misinterpretation in certain situations. Keep it as simple as possible. A simple bullet list under various headings is often all that is required.

For an example of a parenting plan template, check out

www.singledaddydating.com/parenting-plan-template

A parenting plan is extremely important if both parents don't communicate regularly. It works as a guideline or reference as to how both parents have agreed to raise the child. Even if communication is regular, a parenting plan becomes the guidelines as to how to tackle different issues. It takes the guesswork out of decision making and prevents any conflict.

Without a doubt, there is great benefits in developing a parenting plan. Among them include:-

- Ensuring that there is good parenting in both houses.

- Ensuring that there are similar routines and discipline in both houses.

- Provide a sense of security.

- Avoid the child playing the other parent off with regard to common things such as chores and bed times.

- Ensuring that children are getting the same messages in both the houses.

How Does A Parenting Plan Work

Many parents are unable to get a mediator to work together to create a parenting plan. This may be for certain divorces where there isn't enough money to hire professionals. As such, it is important that both of you take time to talk about things. When discussing about the common parenting plan, the following should be discussed upon:-

- **Meeting The Other Parent**. Often, the divorce would mean that one parent would get the child more often than the other. As such, a parenting plan should include where, when and how the children would be exchanged between the parents. This would also include certain holidays. It could be alternate years. For example, this year's Christmas would be at mums while next year's would be at dads.

- **Daily Routines**. This includes daily bedtimes, chores, meal times, access to entertainment and doing finish the homework. Many of them may seem trivial to you, but it impacts your parenting tremendously. You need to also discuss with your ex-wife about the various discipline issues. This includes whether your child is allowed to date etc.

- **Extracurricular Activities**. Children have other activities that they like to do. This may be sports or hobbies. You need to set a standard rule as to who would have to pay for them. There might also be some activities that you don't want them to do. This may be dangerous activities such as skateboarding or mountain climbing.

- **Introducing Your Child To New Partners**. This is a big issue as yours or your ex-wife's' new partner could impact the child. You need to set ground rules about how to tell your child about it and their 'powers' as parents.

- **Medical Decisions**. There would be times where the child would be too sick to be exchanged. Perhaps your ex-wife is a better carer that you do. As such, it should be stated clearly in the parenting plan that when such situation arises, the child would stay with your ex-wife.

- **Babysitting Arrangements**. Regardless of how good a carer you are, there would be certain periods that you can't tend for your child. As such, you may need to hire a babysitter. This is especially if your child is still young. Discuss thoroughly the age where your child could be left alone or when a babysitter would need to be hired.

Although it is possible for a parenting plan to cover many topics, these are the main topics of concern that all parenting plans should cover. At times, there may be a call for a revision in the parenting plan. Like life, things don't really go as planned. There might be some changes that make following the plan difficult. Over time, things such as chores, bed times and extracurricular activities change. This could also change should you or your spouse choose to remarry.

Ideally, look to revise the parenting plan every year. Seek ways to improve on it and how you can help out your ex-wife. Sit down every year and talk to each other to ensure that a parenting plan stays relevant and effective.

Chapter Five: Why Family Meetings Matter

It should be clear by now that for parenting to be done right in a divorce, there should be clear communication between both spouses. You need to be cooperative, coordinated and communicate well with your ex-wife so that everything goes well. You want to make sure that your children can properly communicate their problems so you can fulfil their needs. One of the best way for this is by the use of family meetings.

In many different situations and potential family problems, family meetings can be the best way to solve any problems. Family meetings can be formal or informal. In many situations, only older children and teenagers are recommended for family meetings.

This means that both the parents would sit down with the older children to discuss. However, there are certain times where you include other younger children. This makes them feel part of the group and have a sense of belonging, even if they don't really understand what is happening.

In short, a family meeting is a scheduled meeting which allows you, your ex-wife and your children to get together. It helps discuss various issues that are related to the child or children. This issues may include anything that impacts the children. This allows them to have a say in things and understand the boundaries in the family.

Ideally, a family meeting should be held at least every quarterly (three months). That being said, there are times where family meetings are held monthly, bi-monthly or even semi-annually. This is dependent on where you and your ex-wife live, the number of children involved and the age of the children.

Commonly, there would be a chairperson for the meeting. This could be either you or your ex-wife. Create a list of issues that should be brought up before the meeting. Make sure that everyone has a say in the matter in the meeting, even the children. One important aspect of the family meeting is to have some ground rules. This should be agreed upon earlier before the family meeting. During a family meeting, there could be some issues that require voting and discussion. This allows the children to have some input on the decisions that are made.

I once counsel a man who stayed miles away

from his ex-wife and children. After the divorce, he still wanted to play a part in parenting his children. However, he found it hard because he couldn't communicate with them. They decided to have Skype sessions to discuss various issues but it proved to be difficult. It solved many issues, but it was difficult because a proper family meeting should be done face-to-face.

This is why I recommend having family meetings face-to-face. Make it a situation where the children feels belonged to a group. They want to see that you are putting in the effort to care for them. It provides a valuable visual reminder that their parents are still co-parenting them and are working together to make their lives better.

This may seem obvious, but the entire family should attend the family meetings. This mean you, your ex-wife and your children. Although there would be some children who wouldn't be keen to participate, you should look to encourage them regardless. Tell them that it wouldn't take too long. You should make it short but make sure that you cover all areas of discussion.

There are times where grandparents come into play too. Perhaps they help to take care of the child while you are busy working. As such, you could look to invite them for the family meetings too. They can give you valuable input about the child. This might also include the nanny, step-parents or other non-family members that play an important role in the child's everyday life. Make sure that it is convenient for them to attend the meeting in the first place. This encourages them to attend these meetings.

Make sure that everyone at the table is treated with respect. They should be civil and ensure that any negativity isn't promoted. Make sure that everyone has an equal opportunity to talk about the situation openly, without harmful repercussions. This ensures that the meeting would head in the right direction, where honesty and understanding becomes the main key. Everyone would be comfortable about talking towards a same purpose.

The key towards having successful family meetings is to ensure that you and your ex-wife are on good speaking terms. Once this is settled and both of you have a solid parenting plan, the family meeting would become easier. By then, you can seek to have a family meeting that focuses on improving the parenting of your children. Your children's life would only improve.

When it comes to family meetings, make sure that it is an open affair where anything could be discussed. A great way is to allow anyone to bring up issues which they want to be discussed. This includes certain rules, routines, activities or asking for pocket money.

During the first family meeting, an important

thing is to establish the rules. These rules are important as it encourages the children to speak up without the fear of being punished. Without having rules for the family meetings, there is a tendency for the child to withhold certain information from the parents. Among the rules I recommend include:-

- No repercussions from discussions in the family meetings.

- Everyone should have a say in things.

- No one should be able to negatively criticise an opinion.

- Parents need to listen, regardless of how much they disagree with an opinion.

These are the rules that would encourage children to open up. However, the first meeting should also be a discussion about various other things. These includes:-

- **General Meeting Location**. Where do you all meet? Mum's home or Dad's home? You could rotate it once in a while, but make it a point to be somewhere which is comfortable. Don't have a family meeting outside as other people could invade your privacy. You want the meeting to be comfortable for everyone to talk about the potential issues. Your child would be more willing to share more information about their lives.

- **Will Any Record Be Kept?** There are times where keeping records help. The parents may be too occupied to remember their promises. This impacts the children's trust in the family meetings. Besides the promises that are being made, it is also important to write down any rules so everyone remembers the rules that are being set. This ensure that the children know what to expect.

- **Who Would Be The Chairperson?** Ideally, it should be either you or your ex-wife. But you could rotate it. As your child gets older, they could even chair the meeting. It teaches them how to be responsible and improve their communication skills. During the family meetings, having a chairperson is important to ensure that there is a certain direction during the meetings. You don't want the family meetings to be something where everyone (especially the children) talk mindlessly without any direction and no decisions are being made.

- **Whose Turn To Speak?** Having meetings are tough when everyone wants to speak. As such, you should seek to establish ways in which everyone gets to speak. This could be a simple teddy bear, where the person who is holding onto it speaks; or a simple order around the table. This sharing of attention allows all the people involved to feel that their opinions are truly heard, instead of everyone arguing to be heard.

- **Length Of The Meeting**. This needs to be establish to not waste time. If it takes too long, the child may get frustrated and wouldn't want to attend it in the future. Try to keep it short and to the point. Ensure that all issues are being discussed in a way that a solution can be found.

Basically, family meetings are more than just a discussion. It is a meeting up and connecting with your child. You can look to celebrate their accomplishments in school or sports. Encourage them to celebrate their little accomplishments and it would help their self-esteem over the long run.

What Makes Great Family Meetings

This chapter has already covered many areas on how to make a good family meetings. The previous few pages are about the guidelines towards a good family meetings that encourage an effective family meeting.

However, there are other tips that make a normal family meetings become great family events that the children look forward to. This is a short summary on how to make sure it becomes a success and a great family affair, even if you and your ex-wife are divorced:-

1. **Keep It Positive**. If the meeting is filled with negative comments and energy, the children would be afraid and disengage from the meeting in the future. Talk about the positive things that are happening and look to build on that. Talk about the great accomplishments of any child and look to celebrate them. This builds their self-esteem as they can celebrate their accomplishments with their family.

2. **Serve Food**. My children love the food that my ex-wife and I bring. My ex-wife

and I make it a point to make some delicious food for every family meetings. It encourages them to stay on the table and talk about things in a calmer manner. All my children enjoy the food while we discuss the issues that arise.

3. **Encourage Participation From Children**. Make them comfortable about talking by listening attentively to them. Whenever they make an effort to communicate their feelings, praise them well. As you praise them, they feel better about attending family meetings.

4. **Keep It Simple**. This has been mentioned previously but it is important as you wouldn't want your child to be overwhelmed by the situation. If you make it a point to keep it short and simple, they would be ready to attend them. If it is longwinded and repetitive, they would seek ways to skip it in the future.

The process of organizing a family meeting might take time and plenty of patience. However, it could be very rewarding for both the parents and the children. Start off with a short one first. You need to get your children involved first before organizing longer ones.

As time progresses, they would be ready to be more involved in the family. They would also feel appreciated because their parents are putting in effort to come together for their best interest. Over time, the family meetings become a family affair that everyone look forward too. Both you and your ex-wife can work together to bring up the children, even if the marriage has ended.

Chapter Six: Stop Blaming Your Ex-Wife

In many life situations, it is common for us to blame other people whenever something bad happens. It seems like the easy way out whenever we blame something external. A divorce is no different. Many men start to blame their ex-wives when things get difficult.

From experience, I have seen men trying to blame their ex-wife for whatever that has happened. This is the easy way out. When you start blaming other people, you don't have to be introspective. You don't have to look within and see if you have done anything wrong.

Over time, this becomes a habit. During difficult times, you start to look to external circumstances and blame. It makes us more comfortable about the situation, but it doesn't help us grow into better human beings.

When you focus on making external things change instead of trying to change yourself, you wouldn't grow as a person. You would constantly seek to change external circumstances instead of yourself. Regardless of the situation, the fact is that we probably need to take responsibility.

This is especially important as a parent. The child needs someone they could look up to – a role model. Someone that they want to follow. You should aspire to be someone like that, and you can't do so if you are constantly blaming your ex-wife for things that have happened in the past. Blaming someone doesn't make her look bad. Instead it reveals more of you. It shows your children what kind of person you are.

From the past chapter, it should be clear on the importance of the co-parenting model. This is a model where both parents look to communicate and develop a parenting situation that is best suited to develop the child. When you are continually blaming her, you would subconsciously impact the relationship you have with her.

Probably she is already in a very bad place. But, you need to take time to open up to the situation. Work towards a situation where she is in good speaking terms with you. Imagine a situation where both of you are working towards the benefit of the child.

Although both of you have some differences, you are looking to work through whatever that has happened. Your focus isn't on your differences but rather on parenting the child successfully.

Don't Criticize Your Ex-Wife

Regardless how difficult the situation is, you need to refrain from criticizing your ex-wife in front of your child. This creates deep psychological impact in them. It would not only make your child feel distant from you, it will also impact his self-esteem as he grows up.

Research has proven that children feel bad when someone they love is being talked bad upon. For example, if you talk bad about your ex-wife, it would create a conflict inside the child. In fact, it has been proven that criticising a loved one has even more impact that criticising the child directly.

This means that if you criticise your ex-wife in front of your child, it would be even more impactful than criticizing your child directly. Psychology has proven this and you wouldn't want to impact your child in such a negative manner.

Should your child be younger, say below the age of ten, he might not be able to judge between right and wrong. He would be confused if you and your wife are constantly criticizing each other. You should make it a point to ask your wife to not talk about the other parent when both of you are with the child. This ensures that the child isn't confused with his emotions. When you criticize the ex-wife, you make her the 'bad person'. This has deep negative impact on your children upbringing.

For older children, they should have a better grasp of the situation. They may roughly know what has happened and would ask you some questions. When they ask you questions, try to answer them as simple as possible. Don't give them lengthy stories that would only confuse them. You need to make sure that the answers make them feel comfortable, but that it is factual. If possible, try to ensure that you and your wife are congruent with the answers.

Older children tend to be more understanding. However, the fear is that they keep a lot of things to themselves. It won't impact them on a conscious level but rather on a subconscious level.

There comes a point after the divorce where you completely accept that we all make mistakes. Your wife has made mistakes and so have you. Don't linger too much in the situations. Tell your children that mistakes are being made and that you are sorry. Tell them that you are doing your very best to ensure that they are protected and feel loved. Communication skills are extremely important in this situation.

One important thing is to learn to separate

between the role of a parent and a spouse. Remember to separate this idea that you are an ex-husband from the fact that you are a co-parent. Remembering that the relationship between you and your ex-wife would go a long way of raising your children well. Tell your ex-wife about this idea and see if she could accept it.

You need to learn to put away any negative issues that caused the divorce. Put them into the past and into perspective. This may take some time to adjust but talk openly to your ex-wife about it. Should you have plenty of negative emotions about the divorce, you should seek some counselling to ensure that you are ready to let go.

This helps you learn to let go and become a better parent through this challenging process. Children who see their parents being civil and respectful with each other would adjust to the divorce quicker than when they see anger and resentment.

When discussing with your ex-wife, make sure that both of you don't talk about sensitive topics whenever the child is present. Such sensitive topics might include personal questions, financial questions and issues regarding the divorce proceedings. All these help to improve the communication not only with your ex-wife, but with your children too.

Communication Tips For Parents

When it comes to communication as a single father, remember that there are two main parts that you need to master. The first is how to communicate effectively with your ex-spouse and the second part is knowing how to communicate well with your children.

Being able to communicate well with these two parties ensures that your children would be brought up in a stable environment. Before I give you communication tips, you need to understand the main goal when communicating with each party. When communicating with your ex-wife, the main focus would be for the benefit of the children. When communicating with your children, the main focus would be to understand their situation so they don't keep things to themselves.

These are several tips when communicating with your ex-wife:-

- **Understand The Shared Goal.** Make sure that your ex-wife understands that both of you are doing the best for the benefits of your children. Make sure that you talk to her about it, even though the divorce has made communication difficult.

- **Communicate Comfortably.** Seek a method of communication where the both of you are comfortable. It may be difficult for you to meet each other face-to-face and would need to communicate using technology. Using the phone may not be appropriate because whatever that is said won't be recorded and may get forgotten. The best communication method would be email. Email allows you to have a written record of the agreement between the both of you, and anything communicated won't be forgotten.

- **Use A Mediator.** A mediator would be able to help if the relationship had become too tensed. This may be a lawyer, pastor or counsellor. He or she would be around when the both of you are discussing about anything that impacts the children.

- **Never Communicate Through Your Children.** This is the cardinal sin when communicating with your ex-wife. Regardless of how busy you are, never pass messages through your children. This would make the communication more complicated. If the child sends the wrong message, misunderstandings may exists and make the relationship difficult.

- **Be Tough When You Need To.** There are times when the ex-wife would make it difficult for you. She may lack understanding and try to create problems for you. As such, you need to be tough on her. This may be using the services of a lawyer to warn her or even go to court. As much as this is a last resort, you need to be aware of this option.

The following are tips when communicating with your children:-

- **Seek To Understand.** For many parents, they always look to judge their children based on how they expect their children to be. Many parents don't realise this. Because of their judgement, their children become afraid of opening up to them. As such, always look to understand your children, instead of constantly judging them based on your ideals of how they should be.

- **Understand That Their Emotions Are Running High.** After the divorce, they may still feel hurt from it. They feel betrayed and find it hard to comprehend. They may blame you or your ex-wife for it. Because of this, they may do slightly rebellious. Cut them some slack. Don't be too tough on them. Talk to them to see if you can get them to express themselves.

- **Be Honest About The Situation.** Even though you may find it difficult to talk to them, try to be as honest as possible to them about the situation. Don't try to sugar-coat the real problem, if any arises.

- **Never Avoid Their Questions.** If they ask you anything, be open to answering them. Even if you find it hard to give them a direct answer, tell them how you would give them an answer in the future. Make sure you answer it in the future. These questions are important because it means you treat your children with significance. Ignoring it may make your children feel bad.

- **Say "I Love You"**. Saying "I love you" helps you reassure them that you care for them. In every communication look for reasons to say it. This makes sure they feel worthy and that you are there for them. Don't just say it for the sake of pleasing them. Instead, make sure that you take the time for them and do something to prove your love.

- **Be Patient.** In any communication with them, allow them all the time they need to talk to you. Be extremely patient and don't rush into conclusions.

- **Be Age-Aware.** You have to be clear that different age groups have different ways of communicating. Older children may require more explanation as they would have more questions. Younger children meanwhile would require a simpler explanation. Use different methods of explanation when you need to.

Chapter Seven: Seek Closure For The Sake Of The Child

From the previous chapters, it is clear that your aim would be to head towards the co-parenting model. From experience, there is no better parenting model for a divorced couple. When both you and your ex-wife are looking to parent in a manner that focuses directly on the benefits of the child, great things happen.

The child would have better self-esteem. They

would feel more comfortable in sharing their emotions with others. However, this is easier said than done. The co-parenting model is a model that requires a couple who have taken the time to forgive each other. Perhaps they have understood the various problems that caused the divorce.

However, what if one spouse has betrayed another? What if your ex-wife has cheated on you with another men? How do you find the forgiveness in you?

Perhaps you have put in all the effort into the relationship. You were the one working hard to ensure that your family have the best of everything. You ensure that your children are able to study in the best schools and your family stay in a quality neighborhood. How do you come to terms with the fact that she has cheated on you?

Not so easy. In fact, I have seen single fathers being immobilized by such a situation for years. They find it hard to even look at their wives, what more to discuss about their children. I can tell you that there are many men out there who are in such situations. I hope you are not one of these people.

It would take some time for you to understand, but the fact is that during such a situation, blaming her is useless. She might have caused the divorce, but what's done is done. You need to seek some closure. If that means going for a therapist, you have to. Talk to someone you trust. Look to move on. In fact, you could speak to support group to assist you.

The only way for you to move on in life is to accept the situation and forgive her. Closure is the only way if you want to live your life. Nothing else would work unless you close that chapter of your life. Perhaps you need to avoid your ex-wife for some time.

You may find it hard to talk to her for a while, but after some time, you need to have the courage to talk to her about things. Both of you are still parents to your child. It is for the mutual benefit of the child.

The benefits of closure are not only for you, but for everyone involved as well. This includes your ex-wife and children too. Your ex-wife might be suffering from immense guilt from the divorce. Perhaps she has realised that she is the one who has caused the divorce and look to make amends. Give her the chance. Things might not be the same as the past, but giving her the forgiveness she craves is important.

Closure from the situation also helps your children tremendously. It allows them to slowly feel better about the divorce situation. The reason is that we all make mistakes from time to time. Forgiving your ex-wife for what has happened, regardless of how big a mistake she has made, allows them the gift of self-acceptance. This allows them to make peace with whatever mistakes they have done in the past, even if what they have done have hurt you.

You may simply tell them what's done is done. Things have pass and both you and your ex-wife have divorced. You have forgiven her for what has happened in the past. We all make mistakes in life. Regardless of how big a mistake she has made, it is forgivable.

Showing your children this part of you allows them to know that they are accepted regardless of what mistakes they make in life. The gift of self-acceptance is accepting that we all make mistakes. When they have this gift, they are willing to accept that they are vulnerable human beings. It gives them the freedom to make mistakes without fear.

The Betrayal Of Chandler

Chandler Robbins was devastated after he

found out that his wife cheated with his best friend, Joey. He never expected that. He had been friends with Joey for more than fifteen years. When he found the both of them together sleeping in a hotel room, he was heartbroken and didn't know what to do. Within a few days, his wife asked for a divorce.

Joey apologised for his betrayal but Chandler wasn't willing to forgive him. He had a tough time coming to terms with the situation. But he was determined to move on, for the sake of his two children. His two children were still young, both below the age of ten.

During the divorce proceedings, the court deemed that his wife wasn't a suitable parent and Chandler was given full custody of his children. From then on, his children become his entire life focus from then on. It was difficult initially, because he always thought about how his wife had betrayed him. At times, he cried himself to sleep.

A few months later, he made a decision to get over the situation for the sake of his children. He decided to call his ex-wife to meet over coffee. Both of them talked it over and she apologised repeatedly. She said that she has broken up with Joey and was sorry for whatever that happened in the past. Chandler forgave her and was determined to be the best parent he could be. However, he wouldn't want his ex-wife to play too much a role in their children's life.

She reluctantly agreed, understanding his intentions.

From then on, Chandler worked his butt off daily to provide for his children. He was over the divorce and wanted to ensure that his children would be brought up in a stable environment. He would give his two children the best things possible. He sent them to the best public schools and ensure that they are constantly on top of their school work.

Immediately after the divorce, he even sent the both of them for counselling to ensure that the divorce didn't impact them. It helped a lot as his children were able to have a stable life in no time at all. Chandler is an example of a person who is able to look at the big picture in life. He obtained closure for the long term benefit. As he learned to obtain closure from the situation, he is better able to deal with the other challenges that came his way. He didn't let the divorce linger in his mind, even if it devastated him initially.

Over time, he even started to date other women. The divorce was something that seemed to not change anything. If it did, it was only for something better. After meeting several women, he managed to strike a chord with a woman who seemed compatible with him. Both of them started to live together and brought up his two children. His children loved her very much.

After a divorce, you need to try to look at the

big picture, even if it is difficult. Look for closure because it allows you to look forward to other things in life.

Chapter Eight: Ex-Wife Getting Married

Perhaps one of the most difficult situations I have to go through after the divorce was when my ex-wife got married. I thought I was over her, but the moment she told me she was going to get married, it felt hard for me to endure.

It made me feel like I have 'lost' in the divorce. It suddenly dawned to me that I was constantly comparing my life with hers. I later realised that it wasn't about getting over her, but realising that I haven't found love after the divorce.

This could be a very difficult situation to be in. Many men I know feel the same. They feel uncomfortable because they treat divorce as a form of competition. This arises from constantly comparing to see who has gotten over the divorce quicker. Remember, when you are divorced, you shouldn't treat it like a competition between you and your wife. It isn't a race to move on faster.

There are even some men who find it hard to accept because their ex-wives moved on so quickly. Raymond, from Los Angeles, once told me about how his ex-wife got married within six months of them getting a divorced. It was hard for him to accept that because by six months, he has yet to even get over the divorce. He went into depression immediately after the divorce and his life changed so much. His career went downhill and his ex-wife got full custody of the children.

As the difficulties of this situation loomed, he became frustrated. He began showing his frustrations towards his children when he met them and it became tensed for him. This led to his children not wanting to be with him.

During this situation, you need to realise that making peace with the situation is important. It could be difficult for you, but taking the few steps needed to ensure that you are alright with it goes a long way towards improving things with your ex-wife. This is a critical part in parenting, as mentioned in the previous chapters. Among the ways to get over it, if you don't feel comfortable with the situation include:-

- **Talk To Her About It**. If she tells you that she is getting married, wish her luck. Talk to her about the situation and tell her about how you feel about it. It could be awkward, but it helps you get over it in the future. Tell her that both of you should still work together to bring up the children regardless of the impending marriage.

- **Talk About Future Parenting Arrangements**. Besides talking to her about her upending marriage, you should also be clear about future parenting arrangements. There would be big changes the moment she is married. Your children would have a new stepfather and possibly new step siblings. Discuss with her about how you would meet your children and how things would be. This allows you to be certain that your children would have stability in the future, regardless of the marriage

- **Meet Other Women**. If you have the time, look to meet other women. Date more, so you have the chance to meet someone else to share your life with too.

- **Take Time To Travel**. During this period, it is a great period of self-inquiry.

Look to step aside from your natural surroundings and gain a brand new perspective. This could help you look at your ex-wife's marriage in a new light.

Even for your children, there could be big changes that impacts their lives. Take time to talk to your children about it. When you know that your ex-wife is getting married, you might be uncertain about whether the new husband is someone worthy. This bothers you because he would be your children's stepfather.

If your ex-wife is getting custody of the child, it would impact your children tremendously. Being their stepfather means that he would have his own parenting ideas. This is where conflicts could arise. If you have a totally different idea of parenting compared to him, there could be potential arguments.

Although you wouldn't be seeing your children as much as the stepfather, you still have a big say on how you want your children to be raised up. You need to bring it up with your ex-wife and see how it goes. Talk to her openly about the situation if you don't want your children to be heavily affected by the new changes.

If it is needed, you may even need to talk to your attorney. They could advise you about the various actions you can take. I have seen circumstances where custody is changed hands when the ex-wife has gotten married. When the ex-wife got married, the court deemed that the stepfather didn't have a proper history of bringing up children. As such, the biological father took over custody.

Although this is a probable scenario, you might not want it to happen because it could put a strain on the relationship with your ex-wife. As such, you must weigh all the potential scenarios. For your children, these are the potential changes in their lives:-

- **Having A Stepfather.** It could be difficult

for your children if the stepfather is a heavy disciplinarian. If he is too strict on your child, the child may look to run away from home or not open up to older people. Give your children some time to adapt to the situation. Over a period of time, evaluate to see if you should seek over custody of your children. Regardless of anything that happens, make sure that you discuss thoroughly with your ex-wife first.

- **Having Step-Siblings.** There would be situations where the stepfather bring together certain siblings. At times, they might not get along well and it only brings trouble to the family. Again, give it some time. Make sure that you stay in constant communication with your children to see what happens.

- **They May Move To Somewhere Far.** When your ex-wife marries, she may decide to move to somewhere far with her new husband. This could spell problems for you as you couldn't see your child as much. It could also mean big changes for your children in terms of going to a new school or having new friends. They could have problems adapting and it is critical that you be patient with them.

- **They May Have To Deal With Other Family Members**. When your ex-wife marries again, she isn't just marrying the man. She is also marrying his entire family. This means that your children have to deal with new people that affect them tremendously. Make sure you talk to your ex-wife to see if the children are comfortable with it.

- **Future Arrangements**. Having a new stepfather means that there would be changes in previous arrangement. It may mean that you don't get to meet your children too often. You also need to discuss any financial consideration. Who pays for the children's expenses now? Although you are still a parent to your child, when there are major changes, it could spell a huge financial expense. For example, if your ex-wife and her new husband decide to stay in a more expensive area, it brings up the cost of bringing up the child. It means that you need to spend more on children expenses. How do you balance that? Make sure you discuss this thoroughly with your ex-wife. If you are lucky, you may even discuss with her new husband about it.

These changes are important to consider. Regardless of the situation, look to talk to your ex-wife about it first. Make sure that you understand the situation well and look to work together to see what you could both do to ensure that everything goes on well in the future.

Remember your common goal instead of constantly being selfish – focusing on your children's happiness instead of what you want them to be.

Chapter Nine: Introducing A New Partner To Your Child

In the previous chapter, your ex-wife is getting married and you have to consider the possibility of a stepfather. It may be a tough period because it signals a lot of change. However, things could also be different when you introduce a new partner to your child.

Similarly to introducing the stepfather to your children, you would have to do it in such a manner that considers every possibilities first. This is important to ensure that your child and your partner has the time to adjust. Look to ensure that you have discussed about all possibilities.

Before you even introduce a new partner to your child, you should look to talk to your ex-wife first. She would be able to advise you about things. Look to talk about the potential issues that may arise from this situation. If possible, you should bring your new partner to meet your ex-wife first because it helps save a lot of time in the future.

This may seem awkward, but I have seen plenty of good coming out when the ex-wife meets the new partner first. This depends on whether the new partner would be in for the long term or if both of you are merely dating. If both of you are just dating, it means things aren't that serious and it would probably not affect your children much. However, if you and your new partner are indeed looking to commit for the long term, there are many things which you need to consider.

If so, she would be your children's future stepmother. She would most likely move in with you and bring up your children together. Therefore, she might look to have a say in how you raise your children in the future. These considerations would impact how you meet other women. You would want a women who fits your 'parenting' criteria – women who have similar values. This is important if you place a great emphasis on bringing up your children well.

When discussing with your ex-wife about this, it is important to consider if your ex-wife has married or not. Should she be married before, there is a possibility she knows what to look out for. She would know what the possibilities are whenever another new 'parent' enters the picture. Talking to a married ex-wife allows you to know what to expect. Perhaps your children has acted up upon knowing of a new parent – your ex-wife's husband.

If your ex-wife hasn't been married before, there might be a possibility that she gets jealous though. Like said in a previous chapter, there is a possibility that a spouse would get jealous whenever an ex-spouse gets married. Your ex-wife may say negative things about your new couple.

Regardless of the situation, you should be completely honest about the situation. Tell her about your possible concerns and see what issues she is worried about. You must also consider the viewpoints of your new partner. Perhaps, they are also nervous about meeting your children.

Make sure that your new partner is really ready. Many times, when the new partner isn't ready, they would look to avoid talking about children. Perhaps they find it hard to be with children because they don't like having children in the first place. There are also some single women who aren't keen on children after their divorce.

From experience, I have found that it is better for you to have a steady relationship with your new partner first before bringing them to meet your children. When both of you are steady, you would feel better it. You would know that the relationship is certain, rather than when being in the beginning stages of a relationship. The beginning stages of a relationship has plenty of uncertainties and both of you are just getting to know each other.

Preferably, you should be in the relationship for at least half a year. This time should be long enough for you to know your new partner well. She would know better what you want out of life and you would know what she wants too. This allows her to know your values, what you want from life and how you see yourself in the future.

Letting your new partner meet your children too early can also be dangerous because your children might get emotionally attached to her. When that happens, it makes it hard for the relationship. Perhaps as the months passes by, you find that she isn't who you want to spend your life with. It would be tough to break it off.

Therefore, it should be clear to you that there are dangers in letting your new partner meet your children too soon. These risks could be mitigated by taking it slow. Take time to know her first. As much as you like her now, things might change in the future. You can even look to discuss about the new partner with your child before you even bring her to meet your child. This allows you to know your child's point of view regarding the situation. At best, you should even talk about dating before you start to meet other women. This allows them to feel respected and that you care about their feelings.

Will made this mistake of introducing his partner, Angela, to his children too early. Both of them have been seeing each other for two months. They have been on a couple of dates, but they don't really know each other very well.

Will was a divorcee who went through a difficult divorce. His wife managed to get custody of the children, with Will being able to meet his children every month for a weekend. He wasn't that close with his three children, but it didn't stopped him from trying to be closer to them.

After dating Angela for a while, he wanted to introduce her to his children over a weekend. It proved to be a nightmare because he didn't know that Angela didn't liked children. Angela was around her mid-forties and was never married. She had a busy corporate life and was independent, something Will loved about her.

When planning to bring Angela to meet his

children for dinner, he intended it as a surprise for all of them. His children weren't that excited to meet her while Angela didn't know what to talk to them about. It was an awkward dinner and it became uncomfortable between Will and Angela after that.

Will made the mistake of not telling his children about his date beforehand. This is a mistake that many parents make when introducing their children to their new partners. It can become awkward because children may have trouble accepting that their parents are dating other people. He should have told his children a bit about the woman he is dating before he introduced her to them.

As for Angela, Will made a mistake of not knowing her well enough yet. Both of them were still in the infancy stage of their dating life. They have yet to discuss about many things, one of them being Angela's dislike of children.

If you have yet to know your new partner well yet, don't introduce them to your children. It may only cause problems and awkwardness.

Chapter Ten: Tough Conversations

From the past few chapters, it is clear that there are many situations where you need to be a good communicator. In any situation that you are in, being a good communicator is important. You would be able to understand the other party and that the other party understands you.

Being an excellent communicator ensures that your parenting becomes as easy as possible. Being able to communicate well with your children allows your child to understand the boundaries that they have. There are certain things that they could or couldn't do. It lets them know that you respect them.

Boundaries are an important aspect of any relationship. It is mutual respect of the other person. It shows that you expect another person to treat you in such a way while it tells you how not to treat another person. As much as your children need to understand the boundaries that they have with you, you also need to respect their boundaries.

Regardless of how much you read and discuss about certain issues or concerns that may arise from your child during the divorce, there are also issues that you have failed to realise. You might also have never expected some of these incidents to happen in the first place. That is where good communication skills come in handy.

If you have a great co-parenting relationship

with your ex-wife, you can talk to her and ask her for advice. She may be able to support you in many situations. From the previous chapters, it should be clear why developing a positive and co-parenting relationship would help minimize any potential problems in child raising. However, it doesn't mean that there would be no surprises ahead for you. That is when having a written guideline would help.

These guidelines help whenever you need to have certain tough conversations with your children. As a parent, tough conversations with your children is something to be expected. You may dread them, but they are a normal part of being a parent. They would ask about certain things such as:-

- **Conversations about the divorce.** They would ask why it happened and may try to mend the situation.

- **New relationships.** They would ask if you or your ex-wife are meeting new people.

- **Their future**. They want to know how things would be in the future. This is very common when the divorce is in the process as there is a lot of uncertainty involved.

- **About your future**. They want to know what your plans are. Would you move out of the house? Where would you go?

- **Sensitive topics**. These sensitive topics range from drugs, alcohol and sex. These topics have to be dealt differently for different people.

- **Values and morals**. They want to know what is right and wrong.

- **Boundaries.** There would be some things that you won't tolerate. They want to know what can or can't be done.

When discussing any of these topics with your

child, you need to ensure that you and your ex-wife are consistent. It would be confusing for your child if you have a set of rules and your ex-wife have another set of rules. These are some of the general strategies when having any challenging conversation with your child:

- **Talk To Your Ex-Wife First**. As you make sure that you have a proper conversation with her ensures that both of you agree on something before telling your child. This means meeting in advance or talking on the phone. Make sure that both of you agree about a certain course of action or opinion. This can be difficult sometimes because we have different values. As such, even if some things seem hard to agree on, both of you should stick to the same page.

- **Look To Listen First**. Many parents don't really listen to their children. They are quick to judge and want to form conclusions quickly. As such, they often misunderstand the situation. If it is overwhelming, consider taking a break first. Make sure to understand your child first before stating your opinion.

- **Decide The Boundaries Of Discussion.** There are certain things that you would and wouldn't discuss with the child. Make sure that he knows that. Make it be clear to him that there are certain things that you won't talk to him about because the time isn't right or that he isn't old enough yet. However, you need to be open as possible with him in all situations.

- **Cover All Points.** If there are certain things you want to discuss with him about, make sure that he understands it. Covering every single area of a discussion ensures that there wouldn't be a misunderstanding. Regardless of how difficult the conversation is, make sure that he is clear about what you want.

- **Plan The Conversation**. Don't look to straight away answer his question. Take time to think and plan carefully first. Think about the various ways in which you can approach that question. Make sure that you get several opinions, especially from your ex-wife.

Many people underestimate the power in taking time to think before talking to their children. They tend to get too emotional and simply give a quick answer. At times, the answer may not be suitable or even truthful. Make it a practice to stop and think before you speak. In fact, you could even tell your child to give you some time to come up with an answer. This may be a day or two. This allows you to consider all possibilities.

One of the toughest conversation you can have with your children is when you need to talk to your daughter about sex. If she asks you something regarding, you need to be able to come with an authentic answer. Perhaps you can tell her that it isn't appropriate for you to address this questions. Instead redirect those questions to a close family member like her aunt.

These tough conversations should never be avoided because many of them arise because your child is confused. They may be uncomfortable about certain topics and want your reassurances. If you simply brush aside their questions, they may feel unworthy. Children want to know that they are being listened to and that their opinions matter.

Questions About The Divorce

It is common for parents to get overwhelmed when they need to deal with the many tough conversations with their children. If you need, you should seek to talk things through with a family member, spiritual leader, counsellor or therapist. They are able to give you a perspective on things. Many professionals are out there to help you get through the tough topics.

Perhaps one of the toughest topics to go through with your child is anything regarding the divorce. I have mentioned this in the previous chapter, but in this part I would go deeper into the possible questions that could arise. Answering these questions well would ensure that your child is emotionally balanced and won't overthink. You must be careful as to not give too much information or too little.

Question 1: Why are you and mum getting a divorce?

The key to understanding this question is that the child isn't feeling secure with the situation.

Perhaps he wants some reassurance and understanding of the situation. During this situation, you need to validate his emotions, even if it is negative. Make sure that he is accepting his emotions. He may feel scared or stressful at this point of time.

> *Possible Answer: I understand that this divorce is hard on you and that some situations are hard to understand. However, you need to know that mum and I love you very much. Regardless of what happens, we would still be your mum and dad. The divorce is not your fault at all. Both of us would still continue to work together to ensure that you grow up well. The reasons for our divorce are between us and is private. However, the main thing to know is that you have nothing to do with this decision. Both of us would work together to make it as easy as possible for you.*

Such an answer has two purpose. Firstly, it validates the child's emotions and secondly, it ensures that it is not his fault. The second part is important because many children tend to blame themselves when their parents get a divorce. By telling the child that it is not because of him that the divorce is happening allows him to not think about ways to try to 'fix' the situation.

Being able to keep the reasons for the divorce a 'secret' is also important. Don't divulge the reasons why as he would enter into a blaming mode. He would continue to try to find an answer and this creates problems in the co-parenting in the future.

Question 2: Would you and mum stop loving me?

This is another question seeking reassurance. He might feel uncertain because of the divorce. He has seen how you and your ex-wife stopped loving each other. He feels uncertain about the both of you now.

Possible Answer: As parents, mum and dad would always be there for you. It doesn't matter how difficult it is, we would work together to ensure that you are loved and that you have all the support you need. The marriage is over, but it doesn't mean that you are not our child. We still love you very much. I'm still your father while she is still your mother. You are very important to me and I would work as hard as possible to make you feel that way. I know your mother feels exactly the same way.

This answer gives your child a sense that he is loved. He wants to know that you are still there for him. Giving him this reassurances achieves that objective. Always make sure that you are positive about your ex-wife too. This makes sure that your child don't go on blaming her for anything that happens in the future.

Question 3: Would you and mum get back together?

This question is asked because he is hopeful that some things can change, in this case, the divorce. He is yearning for something in the past and you would need to reassure him to look to the future.

> *Possible Answer: This situation that you are in can be very confusing for you. However, you need to understand that we love you because we are your parents. You are the most important thing in our lives and this won't change. We won't get together as husband and wife but it doesn't mean that we can't have a great relationship. We are still your parents. The relationship between me and you would still be great. We would work really hard to ensure that you are loved and care for, even if we need to work very hard for it.*

When he asks this question, it is important to

close all possibilities that both of you would get together. This is important because you don't want to give him false hopes. If you give him such hopes, he might try to make something happen.

Even if I have met divorced couples who got back together, it isn't wise to tell your child about the possibility. You never know, you may get back with your ex-wife. However, don't give your child such hopes. Reassure the child that you and your ex-wife would love him regardless of what situation.

Final Notes

A divorce would normally take on several stages. To ensure that everything remains well, it is everyone's interest to remain polite and focused on the same goal for the children. Taking the step back before you give any response to a situation is important to ensure a better outcome for everyone concerned.

It is clear that those children who come out the best through divorce are those who have both parents being able to put aside their differences and disagreements. They focus not on their roles as ex-husband and ex-wives, but rather on parents, even if both of them are separated.

I know of no single father who say that this is an easy process. But with continued discussion and give-and-take between you and your ex-wife, you would be able to enjoy a better relationship with your child. This makes them grow up to be amazing human beings. They would feel loved and have their own families despite what has happened.

Divorce is something that is very difficult and testing. It doesn't matter what stage you are in – in the process of getting one or already had one – things can be difficult that you simply forget your children. Don't neglect them however. Things can be difficult for you, but it can be even more difficult for the innocent ones.

Regardless of how hard you try to forget it, you need to understand that divorce is natural. Things happen that make it tough for you to stay together in a marriage. Many couples, for various reasons, get a divorce every single day. When there are children involved, it could get messy. But both you and your ex-wife need to work through your differences to ensure that the children are given the priority. Remember the goal is to bring up happy children, and for that to happen, sacrifices need to be made.

As you go through this stage, I wish you the best of luck.

LEAVE A REVIEW

I hope this book has helped you well. It isn't my intention at all to go deep into the topic. I am no expert in everything. However, I have the help of many other single fathers who have shared with me their invaluable experience.

If this book has helped you in any way, do leave me a review. This helps build our single father community.

If you feel that this book can be improved in any way, do mention it in the review. I would love to hear from you.

I wish you luck as a single father…

ABOUT NICK THOMAS

Nicholas Thomas has helped many single fathers cope with divorce in the past few years. By helping them gain more confidence and stability in their lives, he is able to guide them towards being a man that attracts other women easily.

He divorced back in 2008 and knows how difficult a divorce can be for a man. It was a terrible time for him when he got his divorce. He envisioned his children blaming him and not being able to spend time with him. It gave him a constant guilt trip.

Being a divorced man can be very difficult. Ever since his 'emotional recovery' from the divorce, he has helped many single fathers by advising and helping them gain confidence.

Should you want to share your story with him, you can do so at www.singledaddydating.com/shareastory/

ALSO BY NICK THOMAS

(1) Dating After Divorce For The Single Daddy

(2) Dating Ideas For The Single Daddy

(3) How To Be An Alpha Male

(4) First Date Conversations

(5) Online Dating

(6) How To Approach Women

(7) Mature Dating

(8) Single Parent Support

(9) Coping With Divorce

(10) Parenting After Divorce

Visit www.singledaddydating.com/bookstore/

Get Your Complimentary
FREE BOOK

Join our community today and get **10 Crucial Checklist To Dating Success For Single Fathers** FREE, delivered right to your email…

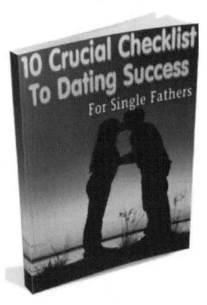

JOIN US AT
WWW.SINGLEDADDYDATING.COM/ NEWSLETTER/

Made in the USA
Lexington, KY
16 July 2015